99
Quotes to Live By

Wisdom from the King

Jelani Daniel

Dedication

...I dedicate this book to my wolfpack, my team, my unwavering support. To my mother, Ercell, who has always had my best interests at heart from day one. To my four children, Tams, Roman the Brave, Super Nova, and Poppa. To my wife, Judi, who has seen my faults yet never wavered in her love and affection. And to the countless friends who appear just when the outcome seems beyond my control, you are the unsung heroes of my story.

TABLE OF CONTENTS

On Life, Self-Perception, and Control

You are told about your destination by someone that does not want you to arrive.

In life, believe in the story that makes you enjoy your journey.

The lowest self-esteem is magnified by someone waiting to control another human being.

They have you hunting the money and ignoring the power.

Someone that fights for everything is just warning you that they do not want to go to war.

Unfortunately, there are people whose sole purpose is to be an obstacle, and it is natural.

You are fed constant negative ideas, so you never get time to appreciate your natural strength.

People with the least to offer investigate kindness the most often.

Capitalists groom you to believe that dead things make you feel alive.

Stop trying to fall in love if you are out of love for yourself.

You are not fighting anyone when your enemy tells you when to be outraged.

Power runs the world and gives money the credit.

On Personal Value and Relationships

How conceited are you to believe I don't like you because of how you want to live your life?

You would understand how strong I am if you accepted how powerful you are.

Dead people don't need your support.

You see the success of teamwork but are taught individualism.

A meeting of artificial people always looks perfect.

You can talk to one thousand people, but sometimes it's best to listen to only one.

Stop telling people to play fair to lose for
your victory.

To be a good socialist, you need to be a
better capitalist.

You can't add heart to your checkout cart.

A poor man's biggest expense is doubt.

You're not a soldier if your enemy has front row seating to your fight.

Teach the kids to have manners, not obedience.

The day my occupation catches up to my character, I quit.

My most dangerous and productive state is calm.

On Societal Influences and Power Structures

Society spends a lot of time wanting you to believe they possess your freedom.

Love shows up many times but is often not seen until it leaves.

When you are rich, society gives you the last warning.

When your friend invites you to a buffet, don't try to get into the kitchen.

Past and present wars have always had a middle person that does not do interviews and reaps the benefits.

Your value can't be a secret.

Your life gets better when you cheer for
your victory.

Stop looking for answers where you lose.

Don't use a scientific solution for an ABC answer.

Make sure your bravery is never missing

Don't wait for someone who did not take the time to like themselves to care for you.

It is not an option if you are not brave enough to exercise it.

Believe life is good until it is.

Real bankruptcy is believing another group is better than you.

On Judgment, Confidence, and Growth

I would never call you fake because that is not my concern; it is yours.

Opinions are very passionate when that is all you have to offer.

I was down already, so I decided to see who was smiling.

Only a person with no true value will judge yours.

Life gets good and bad reviews; death has never received one.

When disliking someone, do it individually and not wholesale.

Everyone loves you when you don't have the upper hand.

Depression loves it when you live as a reflection of someone else.

I don't want to learn to lose.

Manners were not taught to everyone.

Don't act happy, or your mind will not believe
you when you are.

Do not be mad at the people that don't like you;
be mad at the ones that act like they do.

A loser with confidence is dangerous.

Everyone is a character, but not everyone
has one.

My identity is a cheap version of my potential.

A prey forgets that it's taken care of until it's time for the hunter's survival.

On Resilience, Failure, and Overcoming Challenges

Most motivators are interested in band-aid healing, not surgery.

If you are fighting on the ground, you are too close; success comes from a sniper position.

Your worry is your GPS to the destination.

I met some of my best friends when I was down and out.

Love has been homeless but not pain.

My losses all came with priceless refunds.

In a capitalist world, the most expensive life to live is that of a poor person.

You can't hate yourself more than when you are taught by someone other than yourself.

The past has held more people in a cocoon than the butterfly population.

There are some people whose only flaw is their heart.

Real violence is quiet and has a schedule.

Dreams are pushed on the youth but are more needed for the mature.

On Self-Realization and Integrity

When you block another person's shine, you prove you're just a sparkle.

Sometimes the threat is so heavy your only option to survive is to act first.

You were manually taught with an instinct to sabotage your victory.

Most heart problems are caused by money, not diet.

Losing is a passionate sport.

Hunger and desperation are two different things.

The journey includes friends.

When you are required to do a favor more than a few times, it is now a commitment.

To change a sad story, you need momentum; every time you stay still to share, it makes it stronger.

Always remember who was with you when you could not defend yourself.

On Life, Society, and Personal Accountability

Shortcuts have kept me away from my
destination.

No one is allowed to make you suffer for
their healing.

Our biggest wounds cannot be healed with a band-aid.

Opinions are for debates, not for when you're planning to win.

Don't miss out on great friendships by picking and choosing like a painter selecting colors.

Never evolve to the point where you have enough character to judge someone.

Life without some sort of challenges and pain
is often referred to as death.

Poverty has always employed beliefs to do its
dirty work.

Snakes in the jungle mind their business.
Snakes in society don't.

A liar takes away from your intended
destination.

Gossip has surpassed all other addictions.

The mouth gives out forgiveness more easily
than the mind.

The only conspiracy you need to understand is your mind.

Not all riches are connected to an account number.

Do not negotiate your value with anyone who does not have an investment in it.

Your enemy does not show you mercy; they missed when they attempted the attack.

Asking for help is different from begging.

Make sure your friends are not like Montreal streets-one-way.

The moment you decide to ask for mercy is the moment you realize you must fight.

At times, the best thing you can do for a friendship is to listen and not judge.

Use your wooden spoon while waiting for the silver one.

Forward March – A Movement for Change

The **Forward March** Movement is built on behavior towards others. It is not guarded by race, wealth, or education; anyone can take up the leadership. I continue to push the doctrine of helping each other, as it is a natural commitment that is not bought or sold.

Thank You

Your journey through **'99 Quotes to Live By: Wisdom from the King'** has, I hope, been enriching and thought-provoking. If these words have touched your heart or ignited a spark within, I would be deeply honored if you could share your experience. Writing a review or spreading the word becomes a shared victory, elevating both our spirits. Thank you for your cherished time and for walking this path of wisdom alongside me.

Sincerely,
Jelani Daniel